Loved by Yahweh

Cesca Pellegrini

Loved by Yahweh by Cesca Pellegrini is an evolving work of poetic art... art celebrating life, love, tragedy, grief, abandonment and the love of God and how faith triumphs over adversity..

The British born citizen, Irish/Caribbean, diverse heritage Author, Poet and Eschatologist based in the United Kingdom, spent the last 4 years de-constructing her faith, religious ideology and scriptural marriage to her forever love - the army Captain of her soul.

The Poet and Author and Eschatologist explores themes such as racism, the respect for the military, abortion, suicide, unlawful death, social activism, cancer, and nature - some of which have touched her life on a personal level.

Never one to rest on her laurels, always seeking enlightenment, the optimistic perspective of life and love... Loved by Yahweh - ALlah - Adonai - however you personally relate to the God of the universe, the Creator of the heavens and the earth - is the poetic short artistic novel she was born to write.

Thank you for reading and celebrating Triumph over adversity.

Seek to disseminate wisdom not hate...

A note of 'Thanks' to all those who have written reviews and letters of appreciation including the Captain, HRHs, and members of the public....

A Postgraduate in Law and Therapeutics - a life of learning... long may the journey continue...

Contents Page

Poems in order

Resilient ©

Where there are tears - there is pain
Where there is pain - there are tears

Where there is heartbreak - there is sadness
Where there is sadness - there is heartbreak

Where there is hope - there is love
Where there is love - there is hope

Where is faith - there is God
Where there is God - there is faith

Treasure eternity - It gives hope
Treasure hope - it anchors faith

A poem for Iyyob ©

Who am I? Who are you? Who are we?
Tumour growths - am sorry it's cancer!
'What a blessing? What an opportunity!
What is the meaning of it all?
Is it for the purpose of accumulation?
Fake likes on social media?

Response. Heartbreak. Reassess.

A chance to reconnect, rediscover...

Who am I? Who are you? Who are we?
Ditched the religion. Ditched former ideologies.
Is the form of persecution ridicule, humiliation?
Internal regeneration. Enlightenment, Love
Victory isn't a fancy car, house, career
Victory is a state of mind
A way of being - in the moment

A chance to reconnect, rediscover...

Who am I? Who are you? Who are we?

When I look at Iyyob - a man of courage
A book penned in his honour
Purple heart medal won over
Triumphant over fake friends
Victorious over demonic possession
Every believer has their own battles

A chance to reconnect, rediscover...
Who am I? Who are you? Who are we?

Optimism over pessimism
Sign of the times
Always seeds of hope
The second coming
Horologist & eschatologists ready
As the storm approaches

Response. Heartbreak. Reassess.

A chance to reconnect, rediscover...

Who am I? Who are you? Who are we?
Hold your heads up to the sky
Where the stars shine brightly
Let your light shine...Let it shine...
I know why the hummingbird sings
Songs of resilience, songs of hope
Never stop the music, it offers universal hope...

A chance to reconnect, rediscover...

Who am I? Who are you? Who are we?

Wisdom sings softly, So gently does it sing
As Iyyob sighs, the heavens cry
birds bask in glory, wisdom abounds
As the hummingbird sings heavenward
Yahweh answers and all is well...

A chance to reconnect, rediscover...
Who am I? Who are you? Who are we?

Inshallah - Poem for the middle east....©

Where there are faith - there is Allah
Where there is Allah - there is faith

Where there are laws - there are sanctions
Where there are sanctions - there are laws

Where there is mourning - there is protest
Where there is protest - there is mourning

Where there is death - there is dignity
Where there is dignity - there is death

Where there is scripture - there is morality
Where there is morality - there is scripture

Where tears celebrate pain - pain gives into hope
Pain, tears and hope - give way to faith in Allah

Rebirth ©

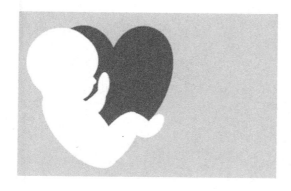

Resurrection - Rebirth - Reincarnation
7 Days - 7 Poems - 7 Interpretations

If a human dies - can they live again?
So asked the gentleman and gentlewoman

7 Days - 7 Poems - 7 Interpretations

Where there is death - there is grief
Where there is death by suicide - there is stigma

Where there is unlawful death - there is courage
Where there is abortion - tears fall in heaven

Where there is life - there is heavenly love
Where there is heavenly love - therein lives
eternity

Racism Reborn ©

No blacks - No Irish
Racism of the white masses
Decades ago

Have times changed?
Have we grown?
Are we stunted?

Racism, prejudice, ignorance
proliferates
Germ warfare, street warfare
Living under a weaponised sky

In enters battle weary bohemian
Intellectual, philosophical, insightful
Mocked, unappreciated, never ignored

Wisdom disseminated hits the news
No longer a coincidence
No longer serendipitous

Racism, discrimination, persecution
Former Captain of my universe
Thanks for lessons in love ...

Pellegrini's Ode to Jazz - Everytime we say Goodbye... ©

Blown away by Rhapsody in Blues
Mesmerised by Monk's Mood
Astounding Autumn Leaves by Jamal

As I look toward Sunny Skies
Inspired by Lady Tee & Clarke
Transported to a Love Supreme by Coltrane

Spiritually seasoned by Salt
Thanks to Turrentine
One Day I'll Fly Away
Sample of Serenity

Cescalovesjazz Pellegrini
Everyday a jazz day
Infused with improvisation

Pellegrini's Ode to Jazz
Chill-out jazz elevates
Memories remain ....

I am 7 ©

I am 7
I am Mysterious
I am Mystical

I am 7
I am Curious
I am Erudite

7 is perfect
I am a perfect 7

I am 7
I am Resilient
I am Powerful
To Celebrate 7

Is to celebrate life
The perfectly imperfect

Don't you try to change me
From 7 to another number

I remain 7
7 defies expectations
I remain complete

You were my former love
Until you tried to change me...

Whispering Angel to the Captain ©

Dust to dust - ashes to ashes
Love returns from whence it came...

Where there is unforeseen tragedy - there is grief
Where there is grief - there is tragedy

Where there is war - there there is death
Where there is death - there are widows

Spouses abandoned - shattered lives
Shattered lives - ties are severed

Where there is faith - there is Yahweh
Where there is Yahweh - there is strength

Like a poem - a living work of art
Love metamorphosizes into particles

Particles metaphysics abound
Einstein would be proud

Resurrection awaits judgement day
Yeshua hands open wide....

Majestic Tree of Sanderstead ©

There lives a majestic tree in Sanderstead
Under whose branches I love to sit and peruse
As the world passes by

Its' elegant chocolate brown clothing
Crushed velveteen in appearance draws
Admirers from far and wide
Simply awestruck by its' beauty

Sinewy leaves, its' wavy bark, entwined
branches in love
Speaks volumes of the love of Yahweh
Bespoke design for humankind

Even though this unfair world takes whose whom
we love
They remain an indelible part of us
Reunited in this place
Nature and humankind will forever abide
In peace and symbiosis

I am Untitled ©

I have no title
I have no name
To many I live as a persona non grata

I am a Uyghur
I am a Guantanamo Bay prisoner
I am a homeless man

I have a title
I have no name
To many I sleep as a persona non grata

I am an involuntary organ donor
I am an aborted foetus
I am a sex slave

I have no title
I have no name
To many I live as a persona non grata

I am a Poet
I am a Writer
I am a Publisher

I have no title
I have no name
To many I live as a persona non grata

I am Untitled

I have no title
I have no name
To many I live as a persona non grata

I am my thoughts
I am my dreams
I am my deeds

I have no title
I have no name
To many I live as a persona non grata

Yet heaven hears my tears of pain
I know that I, you, we
Are loved by Yahweh

I have no title
I have no name
To many I live as a persona non grata

With Yahweh we do not need a title
With Yahweh we do not need a fame
Yahweh loves us from conception...

We may have no title
We may have no fame
Persona non grata we will never be...

Heartbroken Angel ©

Coming face to face with a sniper
Young child innocently gazes
Smoking angel wipes his brow
Within seconds she goes down
Now facing a future resurrection
Soldier, parents, entire world and angels
heartbroken

The futility of war etched deeply on his brow
His wife sat home crying with his and her pain
Respectfully meditating on the soldier's courage
to save others

Collateral damage
Man's wars often pointless
Collateral damage in the soldier's heartbroken
eyes
Islam verses Judaism verses Christendom verses
the world
Striving for peace in ways that confound

What are the things that divide
Hearts veiled and minds blinded
Souls shattered
As the world weeps

I love my former hubby soldier
I love the small innocent collateral beauty
I love my former hubby soldier

Yeshua longs to resurrect her
For now she's cradled softly in Messiah's arms
I long for the day when we will meet
Tears of pain now tears of joy
As we welcome and her parents into our family
United in compassion and love
Man's war is futile
Yahweh - Adonai - Allah is love...

Architecture of Hope - HRH Prince Philip ©

Visiting Sanderstead All Saints Cemetery today
Sun shining down on the righteous & the
unrighteous
Resurrection looms near
Gleaming headstones silent proclaim dead lives
Symbiosis between clay and soil
Miracles yet to behold
Eternity dependent on Yeshua's call
Yahweh longs for the works of his hands
Future restoration to life guaranteed
Paradise lost, paradise regained
Welcoming back the fallen
Past deeds remembered no more
Yahweh has wiped all slates clean
He sits hugging fallen navy comrades
All former enemies of all nations
Finally former hates will dissipate

For the Love of a Soldier ©

Prayed prayed prayed
for a miracle in Sanderstead
On the other side of the world
A widowed soldier prayed for a wife
I never imagined love would me
on the other side of the world
Fearless warrior, heart of gold
vulnerable genius, beloved by God
Loving the Psalms and Johann Bach
Simple living no more qualms
About our religion or our love
Shared love of football
hubby plays midfield
I play safe by supporting all

Diamonds & Champers Love Peace, Love & Jazz ©

Cesca Love Jazz at the altar, Stallion dressed to
kill
Purple & Pink, health recovered, overdose
behind me, sings the Blues
Jazz Pianist tinkling the ivories, Sweet Gentle
Love heterosexual orgasmic thrill

Chorus
Marriage created on earth
Marriage blessed by heaven
Infused with love with mirth

Aromatherapeutic rain, cascades down, no
more tension
Wedding dress, Blueroyale, sunflower in my
hair
Commander-in-in-Cheif & Squadron all stand
to attention
Narciso Rodreriguez & Calvin Klein scent the
air
Flutes with Chatneauf du Pape, I Love
Champagne
Peace, Love & Jazz - Exclusive photo issued by
Vanity Fair

Chorus
Marriage created on earth
Marriage blessed by heaven
Infused with love with mirth

Wedding vows on Google hangouts, agreed the
year before
Legal ceremony held barefoot in the garden,,
signatures sealed in ink
No pre-nuptial contract, love immortalised
sealed by ecclesiastical law
Sanderstead Poetess, unconventional
headwrap, tattoos concealed
Europhic dancing, lyrics vetted, jazz and old
skool vinyl on the decks
The Sea Wolf tamed the Bohemian Iceberg,
inhibitions melt, dreams fulfilled

Give Peace a Chance ©

Singing softly wisdom blows blue
Blue as the heavens above
A monarch butterfly flutters its wings
A Heavenly hummingbird sings
High above wisdom reigns supreme
Wisdom Messenger dreams a dream
That one day in the great reset
In sweet symbiosis will sit
Alongside all living souls
Planet earth restored, made whole
Once more in heavenly love
Heavenly love once more abounds

Cesca Pellegrini LLB MA

Linkedin Profile only

Printed in Great Britain
by Amazon